Shimmer

Wendy Barker

Glass Lyre Press

Copyright © 2019 Wendy Barker
Paperback ISBN: 978-1-941783-57-3

All rights reserved: except for the purpose of quoting brief passages for review, no part of this book may be reproduced or transmitted in any form or by any means, electronic or mechanical, including photocopying, recording, or by any information storage and retrieval system, without permission in writing from the publisher.

Author Photo: Sue Hum
Design & Layout: Steven Asmussen
Cover Art: © Tomert | Dreamstime.com
Copyediting: Linda E. Kim

Glass Lyre Press, LLC
P.O. Box 2693
Glenview, IL 60025
www.GlassLyrePress.com

Shimmer

Acknowledgments

I am grateful to the editors of the following magazines, in which some of these poems first appeared, at times in slightly different versions.

Exit 7
>"Perhaps the Man," "I Hadn't Seen," "Is His Boat Strong," "Or Did I Mistake," and "On the Chinese Scroll"

The Journal of Compressed Creative Arts
>"The Silver Tongs," "Mottled," "Even Tarnished," "The Silver Basket," and "The Trivet's"

The Hollins Critic
>"The Salt Cellar's"

The Laurel Review
>"The Silver Milk Pitcher"

Nimrod
>"The Hollow," "The Dragon Bowl," "Mom's Creamer," "The Scroll's Landscape," "This Far Downstream," and "The Sterling Platter"

Poetry Bay
>"Along a River," "Maybe His Boat," "How a Surface," and "Perhaps Upstream"

The South Carolina Review
>"The Surface"

My heartfelt thanks to the friends who helped with these poems, especially Kevin Clark, Jacqueline Kolosov, and Hannah Stein. And my deepest gratitude to my husband, Steven G. Kellman.

Contents

Acknowledgments v

∞

On the Chinese Scroll 1
Along A River 2
Or Did I Mistake 3
Is His Boat Strong 4
Perhaps The Man 5
Maybe His Boat 6
It Could Be Those 7
How a Surface 8
I Hadn't Seen 9
But Even These 10
This Far Downstream 11
Perhaps Upstream 12
The Scroll's Landscape 13

∞

Even Tarnished 17
The Silver Tongs' 18

The Hollow	19
The Trivet's	20
The Silver Milk Pitcher	21
The Sterling Platter	22
Mom's Creamer	23
The Silver Basket	24
Mottled	25
The Salt Cellar's	27
The Surface	28
The Dragon Bowl	29
About the Author	31

On the Chinese Scroll

a man in a boat

moves upstream toward

mountains—mist, with his

thin back bent, as he

faces the water

that flows from the hills

to the downstream pool

where he casts his thread-

slender line, alone.

Along A River

you will know upstream

from downstream. Off these

sloped banks, clumped water

hyacinths, mossy

strands provide clues, no

movement other than

scarlet dragonflies

flitting the surface,

mosquitoes. Beyond,

a source you must find.

Or Did I Mistake

the pole that pulls him

through the water for

a fishing line? Which

is it? The slant of

his hat, dark-coated

back—their angles as

he plies the current

show how he labors.

Is His Boat Strong

enough to reach

up such a long

river with turns

beyond the first

rock ledge where all

the trees' branches

sharpen, before

the waters deepen?

Perhaps The Man

in the boat is

only looking

down, struggling

to pull his oar

through dark water,

arm over arm,

one lift, one dip,

no time to glance

at the distant

hills, wonder where

this stream began.

Maybe His Boat

is drifting back

toward the mouth

of the river,

or he's grown tired

from the long push

and the banks down

farther lure him

with the fine silt

of easy slopes,

silky tendrils,

perhaps under

the mountains' mist

something hides he

fears he will reach.

It Could Be Those

hills at the top

of the scroll aren't

rocky crags, but

rather ocean

waves cresting, and

the man's boat is

not aiming up-

stream, but down, to

the river's mouth,

which may never

murmur a sound.

How a Surface

can gleam in light,

a crystalline

slice, so you think

there is no need

to go under.

I Hadn't Seen

till now the small

thatched roofs rising

above the left

bank of the stream—

houses, where you

could stop, stretch your

legs on a couch,

a hammock, and

let the river's

current go on

its own dogged

pace without you.

But Even These

stones at the base

of the scroll may

be less rounded,

sharper than they

appear, jagged

edges may loom

underwater,

threatening this

too narrow boat.

This Far Downstream

small leaves appear

distinct—pinnate,

alternate, whorled—

you can see how

they are joined to

the primary

vein, the leaf's mid-

rib, the patterns,

the direction

as they're facing

beyond the stem.

Perhaps Upstream

the water grows

calmer, cleaner,

perhaps there you'll

see down into

the riverbed,

where small fish might

flicker among

crevices, moss

wisping among

white granite stones.

The Scroll's Landscape

is black and white,

the foreground trees'

thin strokes like veins

wrinkling the shore,

but the highest

mountains, adrift

in mist, appear

neither black nor

white, but silver.

Even Tarnished

the sterling bowl's

repoussé iris petals swirl

across its rounded center, but

on the base, a crack somewhere,

so water placed inside—to hold

fresh-cut jonquils for a while—

leaks, staining the surface

of a polished table.

The Silver Tongs'

ends are shaped like bay scallops,

whose numbers have diminished in

recent years due to the loss of sea grasses

on which they fastened, and the overfishing of

sharks, who devoured the manta rays that gobbled

the scallops' predators. Such delicate, rounded pincers

are not designed to grasp anything heavier

than a cube of sugar. Scallops: ancient symbol

of the vulva, primal force within the earth. Around

an oval table at dinner, the way a guest's fingers

handled a pair of lustrous tongs could provide

the sterling moment of an evening.

The Hollow

of a silver spoon, a palm,

fingers curling a shallow bowl.

To spoon-feed. Applesauce,

oatmeal, cream of wheat, chicken

broth. To enter the cave

of a waiting mouth. The bowl

up-turned, emptied of

the little it carries.

The Trivet's

lacey silver ferns,

spiraling tendrils are encased

within glass that allows us to glimpse

the mahogany table's surface the trivet

is meant to protect: the cracks,

the gouged grain.

The Silver Milk Pitcher

on the granite counter

holds one wooden spoon

and three spatulas that rise from

the round opening like arms waving

from a narrow boat, or tongues

pulled from a mouth.

The Sterling Platter

is engraved with patterns

of vines and leaves, florid

intricacies hidden when laden with

porcelain cups and saucers, sugar bowl

and creamer, tea pot, and white damask

napkins, so you don't notice the design

coils like a labyrinth with

no way in, or out.

Mom's Creamer

holds only a few

drops, just enough

to soften the bite of over-

steeped lapsang souchong

during late afternoon tea,

which she spent in her final

years alone, unless a daughter

happened to visit. The etched

oval on the side carries no

image—a cameo without

a face. The silver lip of

the creamer angles

to a point, sharp little

beak—peck, peck.

The Silver Basket

was designed to grace

a small table, for passing

among guests to scoop a few

nibbles of sugared almonds or

walnuts from its shallow bowl, but

now it holds a cluster of polished

stones that for the Chinese mean

solidity, stability, the ground—

almost too heavy for this

dainty vessel to lift.

Mottled

as if with curdled cream or vitiligo,

the silver sauce boat's copper layer

underneath shows through like flesh below

the crackling skin of an oven-browned hen or

the torn hide of a roughly sheered ewe. A boat:

vessel for transport on water. Across the tablecloth

it floated gravies of our holidays. Thanksgiving—

turkey drippings, chopped giblets, white flour. Rivers

down mountains of mashed potatoes. Copper's less

precious than silver, but these days the baser

metal is stolen from alleys and back yards, a hot

commodity now it's used for fiber optics, plumbing,

and anything electrical. How a boat causes ripples in

still water, how the sun can shimmer through

clouds, sudden patches of shadow, light across

grasses of your own back yard.

The Salt Cellar's

no bigger than a kinglet's

breast, one for each guest with

a tiny silver spoon alongside to dip

just a soupçon, a pinch, a smidgen of salt,

this element believed to excite desire,

a mineral that preserves, detested by evil

spirits, this covenant "before the Lord" in

the Book of Numbers, that derives from

mountains and ponds, that accounts for

most of the dissolved solids in oceans,

allowing us to float in the saltiest

seas, and not even drown.

The Surface

of the small circular

silver calling card plate

is planished, little ripples

like a pond open for a friend

to drop in, or a heron's beak

to pierce the shimmer.

The Dragon Bowl

was the one piece I asked

my sister to send when she decided

to sell all Mom's silver, not because

it was sterling because it wasn't, only plate,

but for the sweeping creature, its tail, spikes,

fangs, claws reaching toward a bulbuous sun with

rays that spewed in every direction like the creature

itself spiralling round and round, looping its scaly

body etched and chased across the bowl's width,

this animal whose power for the Chinese lay

in its shedding skin, emerging as a new,

transformed being, able to soar, see

from a great height what has been

and what will come of it.

About the Author

Wendy Barker's sixth collection of poetry, *One Blackbird at a Time*, received the John Ciardi Prize for Poetry (BkMk Press, 2015). Her fourth chapbook is *From the Moon, Earth is Blue* (Wings Press, 2015). An anthology of poems about the 1960s, *Far Out: Poems of the '60s*, co-edited with Dave Parsons, was released by Wings Press in 2016. Other books include a selection of poems with accompanying essays, *Poems' Progress* (Absey & Co., 2002), and a selection of translations, *Rabindranath Tagore: Final Poems* (co-translated with Saranindranath Tagore, Braziller, 2001). Her poems have appeared in numerous journals and anthologies including *The Southern Review, Nimrod, New Letters, Poetry, Prairie Schooner, and Plume*, as well as *The Best American Poetry 2013*. She is the author of *Lunacy of Light: Emily Dickinson and the Experience of Metaphor* (Southern Illinois University Press, 1987), as well as co-editor (with Sandra M. Gilbert) of *The House is Made of Poetry: The Art of Ruth Stone* (Southern Illinois University Press, 1996). Recipient of NEA and Rockefeller fellowships among other awards, she is the Pearl LeWinn Endowed Chair and Poet-in-Residence at the University of Texas at San Antonio, where she has taught since 1982.

Glass Lyre Press

exceptional works to replenish the spirit

Glass Lyre Press is an independent literary publisher interested in technically accomplished, stylistically distinct, and original work. Glass Lyre seeks diverse writers that possess a dynamic aesthetic and an ability to emotionally and intellectually engage a wide audience of readers.

Glass Lyre's vision is to connect the world through language and art. We hope to expand the scope of poetry and short fiction for the general reader through exceptionally well-written books, which evoke emotion, provide insight, and resonate with the human spirit.

Poetry Collections
Poetry Chapbooks
Select Short & Flash Fiction
Anthologies

www.GlassLyrePress.com

www.ingramcontent.com/pod-product-compliance
Lightning Source LLC
Chambersburg PA
CBHW030104100526
44591CB00008B/269